SARAH
WINNEMUCCA
SCOUT, ACTIVIST, AND TEACHER

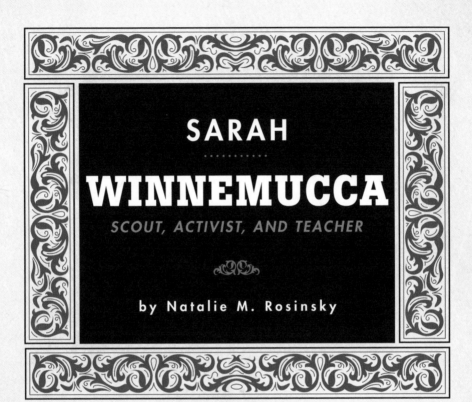

SARAH
WINNEMUCCA
SCOUT, ACTIVIST, AND TEACHER

by Natalie M. Rosinsky

Content Adviser: Mona Reno, MLS,
Nevada State Data Center Librarian,
Nevada State Library and Archives

Reading Adviser: Rosemary G. Palmer, Ph.D.,
Department of Literacy, College of Education,
Boise State University

COMPASS POINT BOOKS ✦ MINNEAPOLIS, MINNESOTA

Compass Point Books
3109 West 50th Street, #115
Minneapolis, MN 55410

Visit Compass Point Books on the Internet at *www.compasspointbooks.com*
or e-mail your request to *custserv@compasspointbooks.com*

Managing Editor: Catherine Neitge
Lead Designer: Jaime Martens
Photo Researchers: Kelly Garvin and Svetlana Zhurkin
Page Production: Bobbie Nuytten
Cartographer: XNR Productions, Inc.
Educational Consultant: Diane Smolinski

Creative Director: Keith Griffin
Editorial Director: Carol Jones

Library of Congress Cataloging-in-Publication Data
Rosinsky, Natalie M. (Natalie Myra)
  Sarah Winnemucca : Scout, activist, and teacher / by Natalie M. Rosinsky.
      p. cm.—(Signature lives)
  Includes bibliographical references and index.
  ISBN 0-7565-1003-1 (hard cover)
  1. Hopkins, Sarah Winnemucca, 1844?–1891—Juvenile literature. 2.
Northern Paiute Indians—Biography—Juvenile literature. 3. Northern
Paiute Women—Biography—Juvenile literature. 4. Northern Paiute
Indians—Education—Juvenile literature. 5. Indian reservations—Great
Basin—Juvenile literature. I. Title. II. Series.
  E99.P2R67 2006
  979.004'974577'0092—dc22   2005002746

Signature Lives

AMERICAN FRONTIER ERA

By the late 1700s, the United States was growing into a nation of homesteaders, politicians, mountain men, and American dreams. Manifest Destiny propelled settlers to push west, conquering and "civilizing" from coast to coast. In keeping with this vision, world leaders hammered out historic agreements such as the Louisiana Purchase, which drastically increased U.S. territory. This ambition often led to bitter conflicts with Native Americans trying to protect their way of life and their traditional lands. Life on the frontier was often filled with danger and difficulties. The people who wove their way into American history overcame these challenges with a courage and conviction that defined an era and shaped a nation.

Table of Contents

VOL. 4

THE SAN FRANCISCO

№ 176

ILLUSTRATED
WASP

PUBLISHED
EVERY SATURDAY

PRICE 10 CTS

OFFICE:
602 CALIFORNIA ST.
N.W. COR. OF KEARNY ST.

San Francisco, December 13 1879

RECORDED AT SACRAMENTO CAL.
BY THE PUBLISHERS OF THE WASP
PUBLISHED & ENGRAVED BY F. KEPPLE & BROS F.

"ENTERED AT THE POST OFFICE AT SAN FRANCISCO CAL. AND ADMITTED FOR TRANSMISSION THROUGH THE MAILS AT SECOND CLASS RATES"

SARAH WINNEMUCCA

Chapter

1 PRINCESS SARAH

~~~~~

It was late November 1879. In San Francisco's elegant, gaslit Platte's Hall, many wealthy and well-educated citizens had gathered for an evening's entertainment. Usually, they listened to music or saw a theatrical performance as they sat in the auditorium's deep-cushioned seats. Tonight, they waited eagerly for another kind of show—a talk by a real princess! Notices had appeared around the city, announcing that "Princess Sarah" of the Paiute people would lecture that night.

Most of the audience knew little about the Paiutes or other native peoples. They thought of Indians, as white Americans called them, as savage enemies. Newspapers often reported about fierce Army battles with Indians. What would this wild

Sarah Winnemucca appeared on the cover of The San Francisco Illustrated Wasp *on December 13, 1879.*

princess be like? Would they even be able to understand her? Long satin dresses rustled, polished boots tapped the floor, and whispers grew louder as the audience waited and wondered. Then Sarah strode onstage.

The Northern Paiute were not organized under one leader. They were 12 or more bands with the same language and customs but their own leaders. The bands traveled separately in their search for food. Sarah Winnemucca was the granddaughter and daughter of respected leaders of one band, the Kuyuidika-a. They would never have called Sarah a princess. Royalty was not a Northern Paiute tradition. Yet Sarah's intelligence and concern for her people—combined with her family background—made her an important representative for the Northern Paiute.

Her appearance and eloquence amazed them. According to one reporter, 35-year-old Sarah Winnemucca "wore a short buckskin dress, the skirt bordered with fringe and embroidery, short sleeves, disclosing beautifully-rounded brown arms, and scarlet leggin[g]s, with trimmings of fringe. On her head she wore a proud head dress of eagle's feathers, set in a scarlet crown, contrasting well with her flowing black locks."

These carefully crafted clothes were very different from those of city-dwellers, but they were splendid in their own way. Sarah's speech was even more astonishing. The reporter remarked on Sarah's "flow of ... natural ... language ... [and] easy, unembarrassed manner" as she spoke of

An 1883 photo of Sarah Winnemucca was found in a copy of her book, Life Among the Piutes: Their Wrongs and Claims.

her life and her people. Her talk combined stories, sarcasm, and imitations that included dramatic gestures. Again and again, the audience burst into "laughter and rounds of applause."

Maguire's Opera House (in the background) opened in Virginia City, Nevada, in 1863. There was seating for 1,600 people.

This was not Sarah Winnemucca's first time onstage. In 1864 and 1865, she had accompanied her father, sister, and several other Paiutes in a few performances in smaller halls in Virginia City, Nevada, as well as in San Francisco. They had acted out scenes to earn needed money for their people. Some of those scenes—such as "The War Dance" and "Scalping the Prisoner"—dramatized their audiences' typically narrow views and fears of Indians. They had little connection to the real lives of the Paiutes. Now, as Sarah explained in an interview, she was on a mission to help her tribe return to their traditional homeland in Nevada. The Paiutes had suffered many losses in the years between 1864 and 1879.

As Sarah declared in a December 1879 lecture, "I am appealing to you to help my people, to send teachers and books among us. Educate us. ... I call upon white people in their private houses. They will not touch my fingers for fear of getting soiled." She noted sarcastically, "That is the Christianity of white people." Sarah went on to say:

> *The proverb says the big fish eat up the little fishes and we Indians are the little fish and you eat us all up and drive us from home. Where can we poor Indians go if the government will not help us? If your people will help us, and you have good hearts ... I will promise to educate my people and make them law-abiding citizens. ... It can be done—it can be done.*

Sarah Winnemucca's audience cheered at the end of this heartfelt speech.

Her words were heard in many cities, including the nation's capital. Sarah Winnemucca wrote the first book ever published by a Native American woman born west of the Mississippi River. Titled *Life Among the Piutes: Their Wrongs and Claims*, it is a story of bravery and betrayal. It helps explain how a tiny, frightened Indian girl became the grown-up who one day spoke to the president of the United States. Yet Sarah Winnemucca's life and story did not end there—or even with the conclusion of her book. She experienced other successes and losses in an adventure-packed life that young Sarah could never have imagined. ❧

2 LIKE A ROARING LION

⤜⟡⤛

Sarah Winnemucca was born in about 1844 near what is now Humboldt Lake in western Nevada. Her name then was Thocmetony, which in the Paiute language means "shell flower." For generations, children of the Kuyuidika-a band had played near rare desert lake waters like those at Humboldt. They made small toy creatures out of mud as their fathers fished or trapped rabbits for food. Young girls, wearing just bark or grass skirts, watched and learned to help their mothers skin the rabbits for winter clothing. Later, when the band traveled to places where stubby pinyon trees grew, girls and women collected and roasted the pinyon nuts for food. They wove baskets from bark and grass to store food and other valuable items. Boys learned to hunt antelope with their fathers.

Explorer John Charles Frémont named Pyramid Lake, where he first met Sarah Winnemucca's band.

When winter winds whistled through the dry grasslands and deserts, the Kuyuidika-a and other Northern Paiute bands added animal skins to their round, bark-covered huts for warmth. As the sun set, families of mothers, fathers, children, and grandparents might see the nearby mountains turn deep blue and purple in the fading light. In winter, snow covered these mountains just as it blanketed the flat Great Basin that was their home.

The Northern Paiute had a few traditional enemies, such as the Yakima tribe, but their lives were generally peaceful. This all changed when white people arrived.

As Sarah later wrote, white people "came like a lion, yes, like a roaring lion, and have continued so ever since." They forever changed many of this native people's ways. Yet their first encounters were friendly.

Sarah and her family were members of the Kuyuidika-a (Cui-ui Eaters). The band was named for the cui-ui fish, a gray-brown sucker fish that was their main food. The endangered cui-ui (pronounced KWEE-wee) is only found in Pyramid Lake.

The explorer John Charles Frémont was among the first whites to meet the Kuyuidika-a band. Heading down from Oregon in 1844, Frémont and his men met Sarah's grandfather near the large lake his band traditionally fished for cui-ui. Frémont marveled at what he described as a "sheet of green water, some 20 miles broad."

John Charles Frémont (1830–1890) was called the Pathfinder for his explorations in the West.

He named it Pyramid Lake because a remarkable 300-foot (91.5-meter) high tower of porous rock called tufa rose close to its shore.

Frémont also gave a new name to Sarah's grandfather, calling the friendly man Captain Truckee because he said this word so often. In the Paiute language, "truckee" means "all right" or "good." Sarah's grandfather, leader of the Kuyuidika-a, believed that the new ways brought by whites were good and

Steamboats became a common sight in California in the late 1840s.

would benefit his people. Captain Truckee later helped Frémont return to California and fought with U.S. forces against the Mexican army there. After the Mexican War (1846–1848), California became part of the United States. When Captain Truckee came home, he brought stories of the wonders he had seen.

These included a steamboat, which he described as "a big house that runs on the river, and it whistles and makes a beautiful noise." He told of buildings that were three stories high. Captain Truckee was most impressed, though, by how white people communicated by writing. He took out a paper he called his rag friend. He explained how its markings carried people's words back and forth across long distances. This particular paper told white people about Captain Truckee's loyal service to John Frémont and the United States. Captain Truckee wanted his family to learn more about white people's ways. He did not realize that, while he was away, many Northern Paiute had grown to fear whites.

There had been some violent arguments earlier over land and river use. But these disagreements were not what most troubled the Paiutes. They had heard that hungry white people ate one another! The Kuyuidika-a and other Paiute bands learned this horrible fact after the bitter winter of 1846–1847. That was when news of the Donner Party's ordeal reached the Great Basin. Perhaps these white strangers might also eat the Paiutes. This fear led to a terrifying experience for young Sarah.

Sarah, her mother Tuboitonie, her aunt, and cousins were out gathering pinyon nuts when word

George Donner led a group of 87 men, women, and children to California. In the fall of 1846, they were trapped by heavy snowstorms in the nearby Sierra Nevada. They ran out of food. Some people starved to death, and others died from illness. Some of the survivors began to eat the dead bodies. Only 46 of the Donner Party survived. Newspapers printed many articles about their ordeal. Later, a survivor even published his diary. Sarah and her family did not realize that what happened also shocked white settlers or that this was an unusual event. For a while, the Kuyuidika-a thought whites routinely ate people.

C A N A D A

Washington

Vancouver
Barracks

Yakima
Reservation

Montana

North Dakota

Minnesota

Oregon

Idaho

South Dakota

Malheur
Reservation

Wyoming

Iowa

Pyramid Lake
Reservation

Nebraska

Nevada

U N I T E D   S T A T E S

Walker River
Reservation

Utah

Mo.

California

Colorado

Kansas

Arizona

New
Mexico

Oklahoma

Pacific
Ocean

Texas

M E X I C O

N
W   E
S

0   400 miles
0   400 kilometers

Native American
land, 1890

*As the years
passed, white
settlers took
over more and
more Indian
land. Native
Americans were
forced to live on
reservations.*

came that white men were near. The women
believed they had to flee for their lives. Yet the
women had infants to carry. Tiny Sarah and one
cousin could not run quickly. The mothers decided
to save their older girls by burying them up to their
necks in the ground.

Their mothers placed sagebrush over the girls'

faces to protect them from the sun and told them to be quiet if they wished to live. Sarah later wrote that she never forgot how it felt to lie there all day, with her "heart throbbing, and not daring to breathe." Neither child spoke or even whispered. Not until late that night did their parents find the silent, terrified girls. Sarah and her cousin had been too frightened to call out in the darkness when they heard the movements of their rescuers.

Sarah's joy at her beloved grandfather's return from California faded when she heard his plans. He wanted part of his family to travel back with him and learn new ways. Sarah's father, a man named Winnemucca, was a respected leader himself. He had dreamed of white people bringing death and destruction to the Kuyuidika-a. Yet Winnemucca could not convince his father-in-law of this threat. Even after Captain Truckee learned that one of his sons had been killed by white men while fishing in the Humboldt River, he did not change his mind.

Around 1851, Captain Truckee set out for California with Sarah, her mother, her older brothers, and her older and younger sisters. Sarah was only 6 years old, but already her life was being changed by the "roaring lion" that had charged into Northern Paiute territory. ᕙ

3 THE OWL-FACED MEN

ɔϛᴥϛɔ

Young Sarah was frightened of the white people she met on their way to California. She hid behind her mother or crawled underneath a pile of robes when any whites came near. Not even the delicious bit of cake one settler gave the children could make Sarah peek at this stranger. When she finally did, Sarah screamed and said, "Oh, mother, the owls!"

The round, light-colored eyes and hairy faces of their campsite visitors reminded Sarah of a scary Paiute tale. This story said that an evil owl spirit snatched bad children at night, took them away, and ate them. The owllike appearance of the strangers had also reminded Sarah of her experience of being buried alive. Only a sudden illness made Sarah change her mind about white people.

Thousands of people arrived in California to search for gold after it was discovered there in 1848.

Sarah had touched a harmful plant called poison oak. Her face and body swelled, and her head burned with fever. Tuboitonie and Captain Truckee did not know what to do. Then a white woman Sarah later described as her "sweet angel" came and took care of her. This settler's young daughter had recently died, and she showered Sarah with the love and attention she would have given her own child. As Sarah recovered, she learned that white people could be kind and good.

This lesson gave Sarah courage to live in a world that had filled with white strangers. In 1848, settlers had discovered gold in California. By the next year, thousands of hopeful miners arrived to make their fortune. Towns grew rapidly. When Sarah's family first approached Stockton, California, at night, she recalled seeing "something like stars away ahead of us." These were the lights of a community of more than 2,500 people—probably 10 times more people than

> *In 1848, gold was discovered in northern California. Because news traveled slowly, many eager miners did not reach California until the following year. This is why these fortune seekers were called forty-niners. Some forty-niners reached California by sea, traveling around South America. Most came by land. One of the major trails to California was through Northern Paiute territory, and thousands of gold hunters used this route. By 1852, more than 200,000 miners lived in California.*

Sarah had ever seen together in her entire life!

Captain Truckee and his grandsons earned money catching, taming, and herding horses for some of their "white brothers." Sarah's brother Natchez was particularly successful at these jobs. Sarah began to learn the Spanish and English languages. Yet, while the Paiute men were away, ranchers tried to assault Sarah's older sister. Night after night, her sister had to hide to avoid their attacks. Tuboitonie and Sarah hid with her, moving from one

Stockton, California, which was the first large town that Sarah saw, grew as a supply center during the gold rush.

25

small building on the ranch to another. It was a terrifying ordeal that they never forgot.

When Sarah's family returned to their Nevada homeland, they discovered that Winnemucca's frightening dream had come true. Many of the Kuyuidika-a, including two of Sarah's aunts and many cousins, had died. Some Paiutes believed that white settlers had poisoned the Humboldt River. They wanted to attack the strangers who had invaded their territory. Captain Truckee convinced them not to, saying:

Nineteenth-century newspapers, books, and government documents spelled the name of Sarah Winnemucca's people in different ways. They were the Piute, the Pi-Utah, the Pah-Ute, and sometimes the Paviotso. Today, they are known as the Northern Paiute. In their own language, Sarah's people called themselves the Numa. This word means "people." The Northern Paiute lived in what is now western Nevada, northeastern California, and southern Oregon.

> *Oh, my dear children, do not think so badly of our white fathers, for if they had poisoned the river ... they too would have died when they drank of the water ... It must be some fearful disease or sickness unknown to us ...*

Truckee was correct. Some diseases that white people brought, such as measles, were deadly to native tribes.

In 1857, Sarah's life changed yet again. The 13-year-old and her sister Elma went to live with the Ormsby family in the town of Genoa, Utah Territory, in present-day Nevada. Major William Ormsby had been a soldier, but now he owned a store and stage-coach stop on Genoa's main street.

For a year, Sarah and Elma played with the Ormsbys' 9-year-old daughter, Lizzie, and helped with chores. While Mrs. Ormsby taught Lizzie her

Genoa was originally called Mormon Station. Lake Bigler, which was later named Lake Tahoe, was on the other side of the mountain and could be reached by a steep trail.

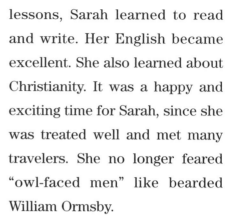

In 1857, a government official in Utah Territory named Frederick Dodge reported on the Paiutes. Dodge believed that there were nearly 6,000 members of this tribe, though he had personally seen only 3,735. Individual bands ranged in size from 150 to 300 people. In the next years, contact with whites brought disease, warfare, and other hardships to the Northern Paiute. Many died. By the 1880s, there were fewer than 2,000 Northern Paiute left alive.

lessons, Sarah learned to read and write. Her English became excellent. She also learned about Christianity. It was a happy and exciting time for Sarah, since she was treated well and met many travelers. She no longer feared "owl-faced men" like bearded William Ormsby.

Yet Sarah had another painful lesson to learn. Many settlers, including the Ormsbys, thought the worst about the Paiutes and other native people.

When two white men were murdered, the Ormsbys believed that three Washoe Indian men were guilty. Washoe arrows were found in the bodies.

Sarah's brother Natchez and her cousin Numaga spoke with the Washoe. The men's mothers, wives, and sisters begged for the prisoners' lives. They swore their relatives had been with them when the murders took place. Yet the Washoe were killed. Mrs. Ormsby would only say, "[M]y husband knows what he is doing." Later, the real murderers were caught. They were settlers who had used Washoe arrows to disguise their crime.

By the time this young Northern Paiute man was photographed in 1874, the population was dwindling.

Sarah and her sister shed many tears during this time. It wasn't long before Sarah first saw the Northern Paiute hold a war dance. Sadly, it was not the last war dance she would see. ☙

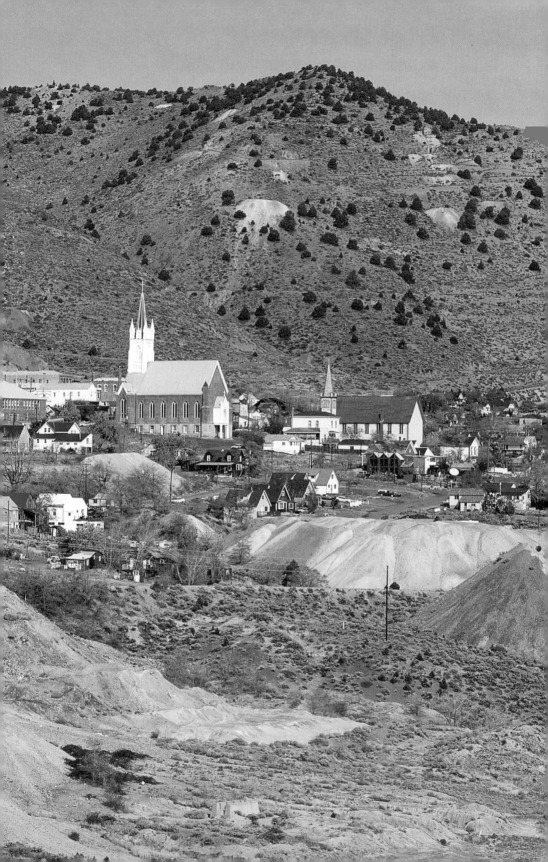

4 SAND IN A WHIRLWIND

Chapter

❧

In 1859, the good luck of three miners meant bad luck for the Northern Paiute. These miners discovered a rich vein of silver mixed with gold in the heart of Paiute territory. The Comstock Lode, as their mine was later named, was close to many pinyon trees. Once mining began, the Paiutes lost a large source of this important food.

Other changes soon followed. Thousands of miners and businesspeople arrived from nearby California and elsewhere. A town soon sprang up in the shadows of Sun Mountain in what is now Nevada. Some of the earlier settlers wanted to name this community Winnemucca, in honor of Sarah's father, the Paiute chief. They had grown to know and respect him. The choice of others won

About 1,500 people live in Virginia City today. During its mining heyday, more than 10 times that many people lived there.

Ore mined from the Comstock Lode was unusually rich in silver. It was worth $2,000 a ton, a huge sum of money in 1859. These riches led to Nevada becoming an official U.S. territory. During the Civil War from 1861 to 1865, Congress wanted wealth from the Comstock Lode to help its cause and not the rebel Confederacy. In March 1861, it declared Nevada a territory for this purpose. Many millionaires also grew richer from the Comstock Lode, including railroad tycoon Leland Stanford and newspaper tycoon William Randolph Hearst.

out, though, and the new town was named Virginia City. Many people arrived who had little interest or respect for the Paiutes or other native people.

The winter of 1859–1860 was a hard one. Many Paiutes were hungry, desperate, and angry. They did not have their usual supply of stored pinyon nuts. Miners had killed or scared away the animals the Paiutes would have hunted for food.

Some starving Paiutes camped outside Virginia City and began to eat the townspeople's garbage to survive. The Kuyuidika-a met with other Paiute bands. Talk of war began.

One voice spoke eloquently for peace. Numaga, Sarah's cousin, thought war would only end in disaster for his people. This 30-year-old leader, also sometimes called Young Winnemucca, was a tall, strong man. He did not fear battle, but he believed the odds were against the Paiutes. Numaga told them:

The white men are like the stars over your heads. You have wrongs, great wrongs, that rise up like those mountains before you: but can you, from the mountaintops, reach up and blot out those stars? Your enemies are like the sands in the bed of your rivers; when taken away they only give place for more to come and settle there. ... [The white men] will come like sand in a whirlwind and drive you from your homes.

A stagecoach is parked at the Virginia City Wells Fargo office in the mid-1860s.

Numaga might have persuaded his Paiute people if terrible news had not reached them soon after his moving speech.

Two 12-year-old girls had been kidnapped and were missing for days. Their families finally found them, tied up and brutally hurt, in the cellar of a settler's cabin. The outraged Paiutes killed the men who had committed these crimes. As Numaga realized, this action meant war.

A few newspapers noted that the white men had been criminals, but many did not. As Sarah sarcastically recalled, the "news was spread as usual. 'The bloodthirsty savages had murdered two innocent, hardworking ... kind-hearted settlers.'"

Major William Ormsby led the fight against the Paiutes. He and about 70 volunteers were killed.

A volunteer force of about 100 men set out to hunt down and teach the Paiutes a lesson. These men, led by William Ormsby, expected little resistance. They said confidently they would have "an Indian for breakfast and a pony to ride." They were horribly wrong.

About 65 miles (104 kilometers) away from Virginia

Numaga, who was sometimes called Young Winnemucca, urged the Paiutes to make peace with the white settlers.

City, near Pyramid Lake, these overconfident men lost their battle with the Paiute warriors. Nearly 70 white volunteers were killed. In this first conflict of

the Pyramid Lake War, Numaga led the Paiute warriors. This chief who had wanted peace carried an unusual weapon—a battle-ax combined with a peace pipe.

Despite this first, unexpected Paiute victory, Numaga's fears proved correct. More than 700 soldiers from California arrived in the next months. They outnumbered and outfought the Paiutes, scattering the surviving warriors just like "sand in a whirlwind." U.S. forces had won the short-lived Pyramid Lake War. Yet the fierce resistance and early victory of the Paiutes helped Numaga bargain to have reservation land set aside for his people at Pyramid Lake and Walker River.

During this war, Sarah and her sisters probably stayed safe with their father, "Old" Winnemucca, and other Paiutes he led to mountains nearby. Old Winnemucca had not favored the war. He also did not believe living on a reservation would benefit the Paiute people.

Sixteen-year-old Sarah was now a young woman and old enough to marry. Before white settlers came, she and other young Paiutes had taken part in a springtime dance and gathering. Sarah wore a lovely new dress decorated with her namesake, the shell flower. She sang a song to the young men of her tribe:

> I, Sarah Winnemucca, am a shell-flower, such as I wear on my dress. My name is Thocmetony. I am so beautiful! Who will come and dance with me while I am so beautiful? Oh, come and be happy with me! I shall be beautiful while the earth lasts.

In Sarah Winnemucca's lifetime, Native Americans were not U.S. citizens. They did not have the rights that the U.S. Constitution guarantees and that laws protect. Unlike immigrants, there was no official way that Native Americans could become citizens. Sarah Winnemucca commented on the different treatment of immigrants and native people in her book. Not until 1924 did Congress pass a law granting U.S. citizenship to all Native Americans, including the Northern Paiute. Since Sarah died in 1891, she was never a U.S. citizen. Officially, she was a foreigner in her own land.

She had only been to this springtime Festival of Flowers three times. The Paiutes no longer celebrated as they had in the past. As Sarah later wrote, Paiute mothers now had more fear than joy as they saw their daughters become women. These mothers knew that their daughters might be attacked. Even the Pyramid Lake War did not end such crimes.

Perhaps such fears influenced Captain Truckee's plans for his teenage granddaughters, Sarah and Elma. He also still believed that the Paiutes could benefit by learning more about white civilization. He realized that whites would never fully leave Paiute territory. Truckee became very ill. As he lay dying, the old chief asked one of his most trusted "white brothers" to see that the girls returned safely to California. Truckee arranged for them to enter a convent school and become as well-educated as settler's children.

In San Jose, California, Sarah loved her classes at the Academy of Notre Dame. Inside its new brick building, nuns taught history, geography, arithmetic, music, and writing. They also taught good manners, embroidery, and other fancy kinds of sewing. Sarah enjoyed needlework so much that she spent extra time on it. There were sunny places inside the surrounding flower gardens where students sat as they sewed or talked. Sarah and Elma helped each other as they learned the routines of daily classes and homework.

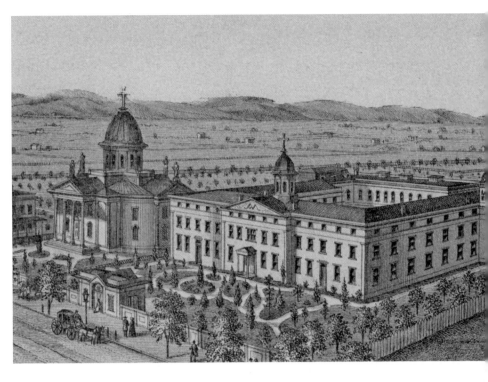

Yet they also learned another, very harsh lesson about prejudice. Most of the students came from wealthy families who considered Indians "dirty savages." The parents did not want Sarah or Elma near their daughters. These influential supporters of the convent school soon forced the nuns to send the Paiute girls away. Sarah and Elma only stayed at the school for a short time. Sarah did not want to leave the convent school, but—like a grain of sand—she was blown by a whirlwind of prejudice back to her people. ✑

Sarah and her sister attended the Academy of Notre Dame for a short time, possibly only a month. The school had been founded by the Sisters of Notre Dame de Namur in 1851.

5 BLOOD OF MY PEOPLE

Chapter

❧❦❧

On her return from California, Sarah found her people facing further losses. In addition to settlers and miners, railroad workers now moved into Paiute territory to live. They chopped down trees for railroad tracks. Two major railroad companies had a long-range plan to bring thousands more people into the Great Basin.

In the early 1860s, though, Sarah's family still traveled by foot, horse, or wagon. Sarah spent 1861 and 1862 with her father, Old Winnemucca, and also visited different Paiute bands. Old Winnemucca wanted to convince other leaders that peace was best for their people. Sarah probably gathered nuts and other food, made clothes, told stories, and played games of skill and chance with the Paiute women. She is thought to have married at this time, but the

The completion of the transcontinental railroad brought thousands of settlers west to traditional Indian lands.

The Central Pacific Railroad laid tracks eastward. The Union Pacific Railroad built tracks westward. Working together, these large companies created a railroad that stretched across the country. They began this project in the early 1860s. In 1869, the two railroad lines connected in Promontory, Utah. A transcontinental railroad made long-distance travel to and from this area easier than it had ever been. More and more white settlers were heading west into Indian lands.

marriage did not last long.

Even though Sarah could read and write, few jobs were open to her. To earn money, she sometimes cooked, did housework, or sewed for white people. Her love of needlework probably made this last task her favorite. Yet no Paiute person or family could earn enough money to be comfortable. Settlers continued to build homes and graze cattle on Paiute land. Settlers camped, fished, and hunted in areas that the Paiutes depended on for survival. Many of Sarah's people were hungry and cold.

The situation had grown so desperate that Old Winnemucca took Sarah and other relatives into Virginia City to ask for help. In Paiute society, this was a respectable thing to do. Giving help to others was noble. Chief Winnemucca was proud to bear his name, which in the Paiute language means "the giver." This is why this proud, strong man was not ashamed to stand on street corners, begging. Yet few whites in Virginia City gave them money.

Disappointed, Winnemucca decided to earn money by appearing with his family onstage in Virginia City and San Francisco. Old Winnemucca was an impressive figure. His nose was pierced with a 4-inch-long (10-centimeter) piece of bone. Onstage, he wore a coat with military braiding and brass epaulets. Besides acting out scenes of what his audience believed was everyday Indian life, Winnemucca spoke of the Paiutes' hunger and other needs. Sarah translated his words into English.

When the Paiutes were able to catch fish, they would often dry the fish in the sun. Large fish were split and dried. Smaller fish were gutted and dried whole on poles.

43

Old Winnemucca wore an impressive uniform when he performed onstage.

Newspapers in Virginia City contained some favorable reviews of these performances. One woman even wrote a letter to the editor. She was shocked that this respected leader had to put on "degrading exhibitions" to help his family and other Paiutes. She urged the "People of California! People of Nevada ... to rescue the Chief, his daughters ... and provide for their immediate wants." She also urged them to send food and other provisions to all the Paiutes.

Sarah Winnemucca as she appeared onstage

This reaction, though, was not shared by most California newspapers. Many mocked what they called a savage "Royal Family." While many admitted that Sarah had a "sweet English voice," they made fun of Winnemucca, saying that his Paiute words sounded just like "Rub-a-dub, dub! Ho-dad-dy, hi-dad-dy; wo-hup, gee-haw. Fetch-water, fetch-water, Manayunk." Such articles did not take the Paiutes or their needs seriously. They dismissed them as just another novelty act—and a bad one, at that. This lack of concern was a common attitude then.

After paying the costs of travel, Winnemucca had only enough money left to bring a few bags of flour and supplies to his people. This was not enough help for the desperate Paiutes. Some had begun to steal and eat cattle that belonged to settlers. These acts only fueled many whites' dislike of the Paiutes. The situation led to terrible bloodshed.

In March 1865, soldiers searching for cattle thieves entered the Mud Lake camp of a group of Kuyuidika-a. Almost all the Paiute men were off hunting. The soldiers killed 29 women, children, and old people. Sarah heard details of this massacre from her sister, who was the only survivor. Sarah

Runoff from Pyramid Lake (below) produces Mud Lake, which is sometimes called Lake Winnemucca.

later described this grim event. She wrote that the soldiers took "babies still tied in their baskets ... and threw them into the flames to see them burn alive." Some of the soldiers even scalped the dead women. Sarah's infant half-brother was a victim of the Mud Lake Massacre. Sarah's mother Tuboitonie died a short time later, although it is not known whether she died because of the massacre.

Settlers feared the Paiutes would seek revenge for this massacre. They urged the Army to attack the Paiutes first, which it did. In Sarah's words, soldiers carved a "trail" into the land, "which is marked by the blood of my people from hill to hill and from valley to valley." That trail soon led Sarah onto many new paths—ones she could not even begin to imagine.

The Mud Lake Massacre was not an unusual occurrence. Invading white armies had a history of such brutal attacks on native people. In 1805, Spanish soldiers killed more than 100 unarmed Navajo women and children. This bloodshed happened in a cave in Canyon de Chelly, in what is now Arizona. It is called Massacre Cave. In 1864, U.S. soldiers slaughtered more than 200 peaceful Cheyenne and Arapaho women, children, and men at Sand Creek, Colorado. The Sand Creek Massacre took place even though the soldiers charging into the campsite saw both a U.S. flag and a white flag of truce waving.

Chapter

6 ENOUGH TO MAKE A DOLL LAUGH

⟋⟍⟋⟍

After the Mud Lake Massacre, Sarah went to live with her brother Natchez on the Pyramid Lake Reservation, which had been created in 1864. One of the first government agents there, a man named Warren Wasson, had been kind and honest. He had given the Paiutes all the government supplies that had been delivered for them. He had helped in times of sickness or trouble. Wasson, however, was exceptional.

Many agents from the Bureau of Indian Affairs were dishonest. Supposedly, they lived on reservations to make sure that their borders were respected by both natives and settlers. But some agents took bribes from settlers or companies that wanted reservation land. Agents were also supposed to give out and oversee the use of promised supplies. Yet many

Pyramid Lake lies within the Pyramid Lake Reservation, which is about 35 miles (56 km) northeast of Reno, Nevada.

Indian agents stole from the tribes they were employed to help. These agents sold off the goods and food that the government had sent for the natives.

Indian reservations existed even before the United States became an independent country. At first, treaties between native people and white settlers established reservations. For regular supplies and a specific plot of land, a tribe's leader agreed to give up some traditional territory. Usually, a tribe's reservation was located on a smaller part of their traditional land. This is how the United States established the Pyramid Lake and Walker River reservations. In 1871, Congress declared that it no longer required signed treaties to establish reservations. Native people lost even that small say in deciding where they would live.

By the time Sarah arrived at Pyramid Lake Reservation, a series of greedy, dishonest men had been in charge. She later described how they would hold back supplies that the Paiutes needed. Sarah wrote, "It was enough to make a doll laugh. A family numbering eight persons got two blankets, three shirts, no dress-goods. Some got a fish-hook and line; some got one and a half yards of flannel. … It was the saddest affair I ever saw." To protest these inadequate supplies, some Paiute men wore pants made with only one leg.

The actions of a greedy agent named Hugh Nugent led Sarah to write on behalf of her people. Many Paiutes were unhappy with Nugent. The agent complained about these Paiutes to nearby Army forces,

A Northern Paiute woman demonstrated in 1911 how pinyon nuts were cleaned in the "old days" of the previous century.

but Nugent only told half-truths to the officer in charge. Captain Aaron B. Jerome, though, wanted to hear both sides of the matter. He had a short letter delivered to Sarah. The officer asked her and Natchez to meet him that night to explain the "very

Sarah's brother, Natchez, was a well respected Paiute leader. His name means "boy" in Paiute. The white settlers heard his grandfather Truckee often referring to "my boy" in Paiute.

bad things" Nugent had said about the Paiutes. The letter mentioned two murders.

Sarah was desperate. Natchez had left very early that day, and Sarah did not know when he would return. Perhaps she could write a letter back to Captain Jerome. After all, Captain Truckee's "rag friend" had often helped keep him safe. No one on the reservation, though, had a pen or ink.

Sarah solved this problem by asking for a stick with a sharp point and fish blood. Using these unusual writing tools, she carefully scratched a reply onto the letter the captain had sent. It said:

> _Hon[orable] Sir: My brother is not here. I am looking for him every minute. We will go as soon as he comes in. If he comes in to-night, we will come some time during the night. Yours, S.W._

Sarah's quick thinking paid off. Captain Jerome waited until she and Natchez could tell him the

Paiutes' side of the story. Their conversation led to a new path for Sarah and her people. Captain Jerome communicated with his commanding officer, Captain Dudley Seward, about problems at Pyramid Lake Reservation. Captain Seward then invited the Paiutes to take shelter at his own Camp McDermit. This Army outpost, later called Fort McDermitt, was 300 miles (480 km) northwest of Pyramid Lake, close to the Oregon border.

Sarah and some of her people were filled with doubt. Natchez convinced them that the difficult journey was a risk worth taking. He did

Camp McDermit was in northern Nevada, close to the Oregon border.

Northern Paiute traditionally danced in circles to thank the spirits. In 1870, the shaman Wodziwob predicted that when a new Ghost Dance was performed enough, Paiute ancestors would return to life. A generation later, a Northern Paiute shaman named Wovoka expanded this movement. Wovoka preached that the Ghost Dance would do more than restore traditional Paiute ways. It would also cause the spirits to destroy all white people. Wovoka's Ghost Dance movement spread rapidly throughout the Great Plains to many tribes. As a result, alarmed U.S. soldiers in 1890 massacred nearly 300 Sioux men, women, and children at Wounded Knee Creek, South Dakota. This massacre brutally ended the Ghost Dance movement.

not let the past prejudice his view of all whites. As Natchez said, "Because white people [here] are bad that is no reason why the soldiers should be bad, too."

Many Pyramid Lake Paiutes set out on the 28-day trip. At Camp McDermit, they discovered that the Army was truly generous with supplies. The Paiutes were no longer hungry and cold. Natchez convinced Old Winnemucca and more of his people to make this trip. By the end of the year, about 900 Paiutes received shelter at the camp.

They were better off than the Paiutes on the Walker River Reservation, where conditions were terrible. During this time, a shaman there named Wodziwob began having religious visions. His belief in the power of the Ghost Dance later influenced many tribes across the country.

Meanwhile, Sarah was busy and generally happy during her

Northern Paiute singers took part in a ceremony, which may be the Ghost Dance. They wore head-dresses with eagle feathers.

time at Camp McDermit. From 1868 to 1871, she earned $65 a month as an Army interpreter and, later, as caretaker of the camp's hospital. Few people could speak fluent English and Spanish as well as Paiute, Washoe, and Shoshone. But Sarah could. She also had another, important opportunity to write on behalf of the Paiutes. These words would come to be read by thousands of people.

In 1869, Major Henry Douglas became the new Indian superintendent for Nevada. When Douglas

A Northern Paiute woman grinds seeds in the doorway of a dwelling in 1872.

asked Camp McDermit's commander for information, this officer had Sarah write the reply. Sarah criticized government policies and dishonest Indian agents. She wrote, "If this is the kind of civilization awaiting us on the Reserves, God grant that we may never be compelled to go on one, as it is much prefferable [sic] to live in the mountains and drag out an existence in our native manner."

Douglas was so impressed with Sarah's remarks that he passed her letter along to other officials in Washington, D.C. A month later, an article about Sarah and her letter appeared in the popular national magazine *Harper's Weekly*. Still later, the entire letter was reprinted in a widely read book by Helen Hunt Jackson. *A Century of Dishonor*, published in 1881, examined the many problems that native people faced.

Helen Hunt Jackson (1830–1885) was a successful writer and activist for the rights of Native Americans.

Sarah's letter was so eloquent that some people doubted an Indian could have written it. A writer in *Harper's Weekly*, however, remarked, "If it should turn out that there is no Sarah Winnemucca, and that no such letter was ever written, its statements will still remain as the plea and protest of thousands of the Indians." In Nevada and California, local newspapers wrote both positive and negative articles

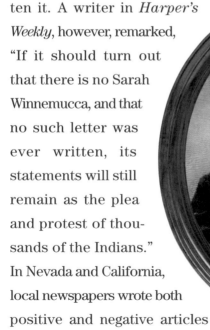

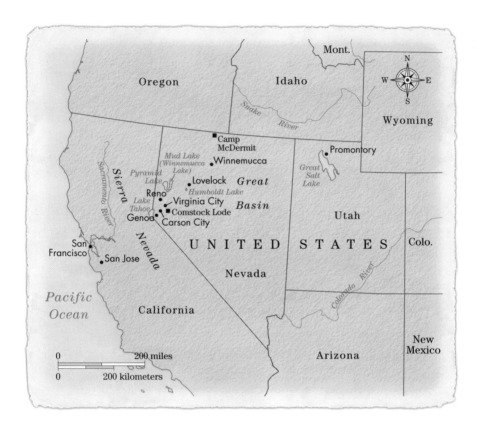

Although she traveled extensively, Sarah Winnemucca spent most of her life in Nevada.

about Sarah. They commented on her appearance and character. Major Douglas gave his own opinion of the woman he had by this time met. She was "passably good looking, with some education and ... much natural shrewdness and intelligence. She converses well ... and [uses] civilised customs, and will as readily join in an Indian dance."

It was not as easy as Douglas supposed for Sarah to move between the two worlds of white customs and Paiute ways. She mentioned this problem in a newspaper interview in 1870. Sarah met with the reporter in a Nevada railroad town. She wore a "white woman's" dress made of fine cloth. After spending time discussing the needs of the Paiutes, Sarah said, "I like this Indian life tolerably well; however, my only object in staying with these people is that I may do them good. I would rather be with my people, but not to live with them as they live. … My happiest life has been … living among the whites." ॐ

Chapter
7   BAD LUCK IN MANY WAYS

❧⟳❧

During her years at Camp McDermit, Sarah sometimes joined other Paiute women in loud, fun-filled ball games similar to touch football. Excited laughter filled the rectangular parade ground they used for these rough games. Often, though, black-haired, bright-eyed Sarah behaved very differently from other Paiute women there.

She proudly rode around the parade ground on a fine Army horse. According to a surgeon's wife then at the camp, Sarah rode sidesaddle—the ladylike style used most often by wealthy white women. She wore a black velvet skirt and blouse, fancy gloves, and a black hat decorated with red feathers and ribbons. As she directed her horse back and forth across the parade ground, Sarah enjoyed the cheers

A Paiute mother holds her child, which is nestled in a cradleboard. The cradleboard was often carried on a mother's back, so her hands were free for work but she still held the baby close.

of admiring soldiers. Sometimes, she even dismounted to their applause and waited for a gallant soldier to help her back onto her sidesaddle. No other Paiute woman there received this kind of treatment. Nor were there many white women there to compete with Sarah for the soldiers' attention.

Sarah was living in two different worlds. In her personal life, she could not always read and interpret signs clearly. This became obvious in January 1872, when she married Edward C. Bartlett. This tall, brown-haired, and blue-eyed former lieutenant was only 22 and Sarah was 27. His well-to-do family had already saved him from prison for stealing from the Army. At Camp McDermit, he was known to drink and gamble too much. Sarah, however, either did not know or did not care about Bartlett's bad reputation. She soon learned her mistake.

After just three weeks, Sarah left Bartlett and Salt Lake City, Utah, where she and her husband had been staying. Her brother

Within a year of leaving Sarah, Edward Bartlett married a young white woman in New York. If he got a divorce before this marriage, Bartlett did not tell Sarah. It is equally likely that he just considered his marriage to Sarah unimportant. Bartlett may have been illegally married to two women at the same time—making him guilty of bigamy. At the least, Edward Bartlett was a liar. He told his second wife that he had lived and fought Indians in the West for seven years. He also told her that he had never been married before.

Sarah lived in Salt Lake City for a short time during her brief marriage to Edward Bartlett.

Natchez had come to travel with her back to their people. Sarah later revealed that Bartlett had been drunk much of the time, asked her for money, and sold her jewelry for cash. He may even have abandoned her before Natchez arrived.

During this period when the nation came to know Sarah as her people's representative, she continued to have personal problems. Day-to-day life was hard for this determined woman. Often, Sarah faced hostile remarks in both worlds she inhabited, causing her to become hot-tempered. Sometimes, she even had fist-fights to defend herself.

In June 1872, Sarah won a hair-pulling fight with

a Paiute woman who had made bad remarks about Sarah's character. Sarah knocked her to the ground and said, "There, talk so about me to white folks, will you!" Just a few weeks later, Sarah was involved in what a local newspaper sarcastically described as "A BLOODY COMBAT." Sarah had given a hotel waiter who had insulted her a black eye. He, in turn, split Sarah's lip during this fight. Some papers were eager to report any news that cast a bad light on the Paiute woman they still distrusted because of her race.

In 1875, there was more news to report. In the rough railroad town of Winnemucca, Sarah had successfully defended herself from attack by a white man. He had tried to force his way into her home. Sarah fought back, using a penknife to cut

A Paiute encampment had traditional dwellings as well as canvas tents.

his face. She was arrested and held in jail. Many Paiutes feared that Sarah would never receive a fair hearing in the white people's courts. This streak of bad luck ended, though, when an influential lawyer volunteered to help her. He brought many witnesses to speak for her good character and trustworthiness. Sarah was set free.

Later that year, Sarah's life took a new direction. She joined her father, his band of Paiutes, and others at Malheur Reservation in southeastern Oregon. Sarah was hired as the reservation's interpreter. Their first years there were good ones. Then the Paiutes might have laughed to hear that malheur means "bad luck" in French.

Samuel B. Parrish, the Indian agent at Malheur Reservation, was kind, honest, and fair. He distributed all government supplies and helped the Paiutes there plant crops and construct buildings. His sister-in-law Annie, with Sarah's help, taught the Paiute children English. Sarah later recalled that her

Samuel B. Parrish was the son of Methodist missionaries in Oregon. He treated the Paiutes well.

people called this gentle woman their "white lily mother." After hearing what Malheur Reservation was like, other Paiutes traveled there. By the end of 1875, nearly 750 Paiutes lived at Malheur. Yet a new government policy dramatically altered their lives.

A man named William Rinehart replaced Samuel Parrish as Malheur's Indian agent. Even though Sarah's people desperately wanted the Parrishes to stay, the Paiutes had no say in this matter. This transfer of power was a major stroke of bad luck. Rinehart's cruel nature and prejudiced beliefs were obvious.

William Rinehart was a former Army major who had fought the Indians in Oregon and continued to think of them as the enemy.

Sarah later described how he picked up a small Paiute boy by the ear, threw him against a wall, and then kicked him. Rinehart told her that he did it because the "little devil laughed at me." Rinehart did not care that the boy did not understand English. He expected immediate obedience from all the Paiutes.

Rinehart did not distribute supplies fairly. His harsh and brutal behavior toward young, defenseless people continued. Some Paiutes began to leave Malheur Reservation and headed to the nearby mountains in hopes of finding shelter and food. Chief Winnemucca was among those who left. In an official report, an outraged Rinehart wrote that Indians "roam the country at will in defiance of the wishes of the whites."

Outspoken Sarah had a number of conflicts with Rinehart. Yet she did not leave Malheur Reservation when her father did. During these difficult months, Sarah had met and fallen in love with a man named Joseph Satwaller. Sarah got an official divorce from Edward Bartlett. In November 1876, the 32-year-old Sarah married Satwaller in the home of her friend, Annie Parrish. Their marriage was listed in the records of the local courthouse. Little more is known for certain about Sarah's new husband.

The couple lived outside the Malheur Reservation. Yet this marriage also proved an unsuccessful one for Sarah. The pair separated sometime before June 1878. That is when this brave, strong woman went into battle for her people.

> *Under President Ulysses S. Grant, the Bureau of Indian Affairs changed its staff. Many members of religious organizations replaced existing Indian agents on reservations. It was during this changeover that brutal William Rinehart replaced Samuel Parrish at Malheur Reservation.*

8 WORTHY OF BEING A CHIEF

Chapter

ᕉᕉᕉ

In 1878, the Bannock people of southern Idaho had taken up arms against the whites. This tribe of 1,000 people spoke the same language as the Northern Paiute, but traditionally they were more aggressive. Bannock warriors proudly wore moccasins dyed red to show that they stepped in the blood of their enemies. The Bannocks hunted buffalo, and they mockingly called Sarah's people timid rabbit hunters.

Still, the Bannocks had found themselves in difficulties similar to the Paiutes'. Whites had killed off most buffalo. Settlers' livestock had destroyed the fields of camas roots, another major food for the Bannocks. Greedy Indian agents had withheld supplies that the Bannocks had been promised in treaties. The Bannocks were slowly starving. Now, as in the Pyramid Lake War, tensions exploded when whites assaulted a young native girl.

Winnemucca, Natchez, and other members of the Kuyuidika-a were trapped inside the main Bannock camp when war erupted. Winnemucca had gone there as a peacemaker, hoping to convince the Bannocks that it was in their own best interest not to fight. Now, they could not leave without seeming to betray the Bannocks, whose war chiefs hoped to persuade all the Paiutes to become Bannock allies in this war. Winnemucca also worried that whites might believe that his band had indeed joined the Bannocks.

Oliver O. Howard (1830–1909) was known as the "praying general" for his strong moral beliefs. He treated blacks and Native Americans with respect, and helped found Howard University, a traditionally black college in Washington, D.C. It was named in his honor.

Meanwhile, General Oliver O. Howard, who was in charge of the soldiers fighting this war, asked Sarah to be his official interpreter. He also told her about Winnemucca's problem. He said the Army would welcome the Kuyuidika-a back once they returned. Sarah agreed to work not only as an interpreter but also as a scout. Accompanied only by two other Paiute men, she set off on the danger-

ous and exhausting mission of traveling 220 miles (352 km) by horse to rescue her trapped people.

She did not use her fashionable lady's sidesaddle for this difficult trip. To reach the Bannock camp quickly, she rode almost nonstop for three days and nights. She later wrote that "[t]his was the hardest work I ever did for the government in all my life." When Sarah and her companions neared the Bannock camp, they discovered just

A drawing of Sarah on an Army mission appeared in an Oregon newspaper in 1906. The newspaper called her the "Pacific Coast Pocahontas."

An illustration of a group of Bannock Indians appeared in Harper's Weekly in 1878. It was made from a photograph by William Henry Jackson.

how large a challenge they faced. There were more than 325 lodges and 450 Bannock warriors surrounding the Paiutes there. Sarah did not let fear stop her. She disguised herself by trading her fancy riding outfit for native gear. She loosened her curled hair, dabbed paint on her face, and wrapped herself in a blanket.

Sarah quietly sneaked into the camp, found Winnemucca, and told him about General Howard's welcome. She helped Winnemucca plan how the Paiutes would escape while pretending to go about their daily routines. The next day, their plan succeeded. Sarah had reason to feel proud when, several years later, she wrote that "I, only an Indian woman, went and saved my father and his people." Winnemucca himself praised Sarah. Later, when all his people had gathered together, he stood to announce that "hereafter we will look upon her as our chieftain, for none of us are worthy of being chief but her."

The Paiutes did, in fact, respect Sarah's abilities. But by year's end, after U.S. forces defeated the Bannocks, the Paiutes found themselves facing even greater problems. They desperately turned to Sarah as well as their traditional leader Winnemucca for help.

The U.S. government had ordered that all Indians involved in the Bannock War be sent to the Yakima Reservation in Washington state. Not only were the defeated Bannocks being forced to go, but the Paiutes were being sent there as well—even though only a few Paiutes had fought alongside the Bannocks.

In 1804, the U.S. government began to forcibly remove some tribes from their traditional territories. This policy was first used with native people in the Southeastern states. The Cherokee, Chickasaw, Choctaw, and Creek people were made to move far away. Their new homes were reservations in the "Indian Territory" that later became Oklahoma. Many native people died on brutal forced marches to their unwanted new homes. Whites then used the rich lands that these tribes had been forced to abandon. Another Great Basin tribe, the Modoc people, was forced to leave their traditional land in the Great Basin in 1873.

The Northern Paiute were forced to leave their traditional homelands in the Sierra Nevada.

It did not matter to the U.S. government that most Paiutes had been bystanders. It also did not trouble the government that the Yakima Reservation was far from the Paiutes' traditional territory. For many years, the United States had been forcibly removing native peoples far from their homes.

Sarah was horrified. This order was not only unjust but also a death sentence for some Paiutes. It was midwinter, and they were to travel 350 miles

(560 km) northward through snow-covered mountains. She wondered about the nature of a U.S. president who would condemn people to die for no reason. Sarah recalled asking "whether he is made of wood or rock, for … [n]o human being would do such a thing as that."

At night, she would imagine the president as a "thing" with "big eyes and long legs, and a head like a bull-frog or something like that."

Sarah could not persuade Army officers to disregard these harsh orders. She accompanied her people on their bitter journey northward. She saw infants, new mothers, and old people die during the monthlong march. When the Paiutes finally arrived at Yakima, Sarah also witnessed their unfriendly reception. The current inhabitants of the Yakima Reservation were the Yakima people, traditional enemies of the Paiutes. The Indian agent, a cold-hearted man named James Wilbur, had not even known the Paiutes were coming. He grudgingly had an unheated shed built for them.

In 1879, another Native American woman began lecturing about her people's needs. Susette La Flesche was a member of the Omaha tribe in Nebraska. She was known as "Bright Eyes," the English translation of her Omaha name. The well-educated Bright Eyes first spoke out about the forced removal of a neighboring tribe, the Ponca, to Indian Territory. Later, she wrote articles for newspapers and magazines. Her sister, Susan La Flesche Picotte, was the first Native American woman doctor.

Two Paiute women and their children were photographed in about 1874.

There, like cattle typically herded into such places, the desperate Paiutes huddled together for warmth.

When spring came, the surviving Paiutes learned how much Wilbur was like the despised Agent Rinehart at Malheur. Wilbur distributed too few supplies. This religious man did not even let the Paiutes keep the wheat they grew that year. His limited idea of Christianity did not include such fairness or kindness to non-Christians. Instead, Wilbur gave their crop and other goods to the Yakima people he had converted to Christianity. Sarah later bitterly told this religious hypocrite that "hell is full of just such Christians as you are."

Desperate for relief, Sarah's people asked her to visit the "Great White Father" in Washington, D.C. Soldiers and Indian agents always said they acted on his orders. If Sarah could explain their needs to the president of the United States, perhaps they could return to their own territory.

Sarah agreed. First, though, she gave a series of lectures in San Francisco about the Paiutes' problems. Sarah hoped to gain support from these 1879 appearances. She also wanted to be as strong as possible when she finally met that mysterious, frighteningly powerful figure, the president. ℘

9 I Am Crying Out ... for Justice

⸙⸙⸙

In January 1880, Sarah, her father Winnemucca, her brother Natchez, and another Paiute leader, Captain Jim, traveled to Washington, D.C. Riding the transcontinental railroad, they completed this journey in a week. A Bureau of Indian Affairs official met and escorted them during their stay. Sarah and her people wore their best "white man's" clothing throughout this visit.

Sarah talked at length with Secretary of the Interior Carl Schurz. She translated Winnemucca's and Natchez's words, and Schurz seemed sympathetic to their concerns. He even agreed to write a letter stating that the Paiutes should be permitted to return to their Great Basin homeland. Sarah's joy at this success balanced out the disappointingly brief

Sarah Winnemucca sometimes wore a black velvet costume instead of the more traditional buckskin dress during her lectures about her Paiute people.

meeting with the president that followed.

Broad-shouldered, bearded Rutherford B. Hayes paused only for a minute as he passed Sarah in a White House waiting room. After shaking hands, Hayes asked, "Did you get all you want for your people?" Sarah replied, "Yes, sir, as far as I know." As Sarah later recalled, Hayes responded, "That is well" and then he left the room. This meeting was very different from the frightening things Sarah had once imagined about the president.

Yet there was more than enough emotion upon Sarah's return to Yakima. At first, she and her people

The delegation to Washington, D.C., included (from left) Sarah, Old Winnemucca, Natchez, and Captain Jim, a Paiute chief.

excitedly waited for supplies Schurz had promised. Then she asked Wilbur when the Paiutes might leave for their traditional home. But he had received no official notice of this. Furthermore, Wilbur refused to act on the letter from Schurz that Sarah herself had carried back with her.

Sarah sent this photograph to her brother, Natchez. She is wearing a medal Natchez received after the Bannock War.

At first, the Paiutes were angry with the government and Wilbur. Later, some of them began to believe that Sarah might have lied to them. Some Paiutes even thought she might have taken money to betray them. Their distrust wounded Sarah as deeply as any bullet. As she tried to explain, "I know I have told you more lies than I have hair on my head. I tell you ... they were the words of the white people, not mine." Sarah realized bitterly that this attempt to rescue her people had failed.

Unwelcome at Yakima, Sarah moved 60 miles (96 km) away to the Vancouver Barracks. There, she worked for the Army as a teacher of Indian children and prisoners. Official reports praised her for her successful teaching.

In December 1881, Sarah married former Army Lieutenant Lewis H. Hopkins in San Francisco. Thirty-seven-year-old Sarah might have first met this brown-haired, younger man during the Bannock War. They might have just met during Sarah's recent visit with her sister Elma in Montana. However they became acquainted, romantic Sarah had made another poor choice. Hopkins dressed elegantly and wore a fashionable handlebar mustache. His attractive appearance, though, hid many character flaws.

Sarah's new husband drank and gambled. He spent most of the $500 Sarah had finally received for her earlier work as a scout. For a year, Hopkins' troubling behavior delayed a project that Sarah was eager to begin. She now had another opportunity to help her people.

Sarah was to tour the Northeast, giving a series of lectures about her people. She would explain the Paiutes' needs for land, food, and rights under the law. Two sisters from Boston, Elizabeth Peabody and Mary

Elizabeth Peabody spread the German system of educating young children throughout the United States. This method kept its original name of kindergarten. In the German language, this word means "children's garden." Mary Peabody Mann was also a teacher as well as a writer. These sisters worked for the antislavery movement, women's rights, and native people's rights. Their lifelong membership in the Unitarian Church was important to both of these remarkable women.

Elizabeth Peabody (1804–1894) was a strong supporter of Sarah.

Peabody Mann, might have arranged this tour. These elderly women had a long history of working for social change. When Sarah finally arrived in the spring of 1883, the three women became close. Sarah often stayed in Elizabeth's home instead of a hotel.

Sarah spoke to large church groups and other gatherings in New York, Connecticut, Rhode Island,

In 1887, Senator Henry L. Dawes' work on behalf of native people became law. At the time, both Sarah Winnemucca and Bright Eyes agreed that the Dawes Allotment Act would help all tribes. They supported the Massachusetts senator's efforts. The women later realized that they had been very wrong. The act gave each adult male in a tribe 160 acres (65 hectares) of its reservation land. Once this land was portioned out, though, the remainder became available for use by whites. The act actually reduced the amount of promised reservation land that tribes held. It also weakened the ties between tribe members.

Maryland, Massachusetts, and Pennsylvania. She gave more than 300 lectures. People were more than willing to pay the 10- to 25-cent admission charge to hear her speak. Sarah and her husband used these fees to help pay their living expenses. Hopkins often appeared onstage to introduce his wife. At these lectures, Sarah would wear a buckskin dress with beaded jewelry—clothing typically worn by better known Great Plains native people rather than the Paiutes. Sometimes she added a small gold crown and fashionably embroidered bag to her costume.

Many influential people came to hear her speak. These included Senator Henry L. Dawes of Massachusetts, who later sponsored a law that changed the lives of many native people. Women at Sarah's lectures were eager to hear about how the Paiutes married and raised children. When Mary Peabody Mann suggested that Sarah write a book, Sarah realized that this might be a wonderful way to

PETITION

To the Honorable Congress of the United States.

Whereas, the tribe of Piute Indians that formerly occupied the greater part of Nevada and now diminished by its sufferings and wrongs to one-third of its original number, has always kept its promise of peace and friendliness to the whites since they first entered their country, and has of late been deprived of the Malheur Reservation decreed to them by President Grant:

I, Sarah Winnemucca Hopkins, granddaughter of Captain Truckee, who promised friendship for his tribe to General Fremont, whom he guided into California and served through the Mexican war—together with the undersigned friends who sympathize in the cause of my people—do petition the Honorable Congress of the United States to restore to them said Malheur Reservation, which is well watered and timbered, and large enough to afford homes and support for them all, where they can enjoy lands in severalty without loosing their tribal relations, so essential to their happiness and good character, and where their citizenship, implied in this distribution of land, will defend them from the encroachments of the white settlers, so detrimental to their interest and their virtues. And especially do we petition for the return of that portion of the tribe arbitrarily removed from the Malheur Reservation, after the Bannock war, to the Yakima Reservation, on Columbia River, in which removal families were ruthlessly separated, and have never ceased to pine for husbands, wives, and children, which restoration was pledged to them by the Secretary of the Interior in 1880, but has not been fulfilled.

Boston Dec. 1883

[Signatures]

Sarah circulated petitions in support of the Paiutes during her lectures.

reach even more people with her message. Mary offered to correct spelling errors and arrange for publication. Lewis researched facts in libraries. Late in 1883, Sarah Winnemucca's *Life Among the Piutes: Their Wrongs and Claims* appeared in print.

LIFE AMONG THE PIUTES:

Their Wrongs and Claims.

BY

SARAH WINNEMUCCA HOPKINS.

EDITED BY

MRS. HORACE MANN,

AND

PRINTED FOR THE AUTHOR.

BOSTON:
FOR SALE BY CUPPLES, UPHAM & CO.
283 WASHINGTON STREET;
G. P. PUTNAM'S SONS, NEW YORK;
AND BY THE AUTHOR.
1883.

This eight-chapter, leather-bound book sold for $1 a copy. It concluded with many letters from Nevada citizens and Army officers who praised Sarah's good character. Mary and Sarah hoped these letters would offset bad remarks being made by members of the Bureau of Indian Affairs. People such as William Rinehart resented Sarah's criticism of Indian agents and the reservation system. They hoped people would stop listening to Sarah if they believed she was dishonest.

Sarah poured her heart and soul into her book. She wrote directly to those who had hurt her people but still had the power to help them. She begged, saying:

> *Oh, for shame! ... [Y]ou, who call yourselves the great civilization; you ... who have [pledged] with God to make this land the home of the free and the brave. ... I am crying out to you for justice—yes, pleading for the far-off plains of the West for ... my people.*

The success of her lecture tour and her book led Sarah to hope that her cries would finally be heard. Yet, once again, Sarah Winnemucca returned home only to face old disappointments and new challenges.

In her book, Sarah Winnemucca sometimes gives the wrong dates for historical events. She mixes up the order of a few incidents. At the same time, she includes word-for-word whole speeches and conversations held long ago. Is her memory trustworthy? One historian points out that using exact dates was not a Paiute tradition. In addition, the Paiutes memorized and spoke all their history and stories instead of writing them. As the close relative of tribal leaders, Sarah was especially skilled in remembering what was said at important meetings. Her background makes her detailed recollection of speeches and conversations believable.

Chapter

10 THE CHIEFTAIN'S WEARY DAUGHTER

❧

Returning to Nevada in 1884, Sarah needed money. Her husband had gambled and drank away some of their savings. Sarah had lent the rest to her brother Natchez. But Indian agents refused to hire her as a reservation interpreter or teacher because she had criticized them. When Sarah tried to earn money by lecturing in Reno and Carson City, few people came to her talks. Sarah began to question how much good her book and lectures had actually accomplished.

Sarah felt pain for another reason. Many Paiutes continued to distrust her. Even though she was now short of cash, they knew that Sarah lived well at other times. She had lived like the whites while the Paiutes suffered. After a year filled with these struggles, Sarah voiced her painful conclusion. She told a

A statue of Sarah Winnemucca sits outside the Capitol in Washington, D.C., before taking its place in Statuary Hall.

local newspaper reporter that she was abandoning "the fight. … I have worked for freedom. I have labored to give my race a voice in the affairs of the nation, but they prefer to be slaves so let it be." At this low point in her life, Sarah was emotionally worn out—in her own words, just "the chieftain's weary daughter" who thought death might be peaceful.

During this time, Sarah and her husband separated. This parting added to her sadness. Yet Sarah overcame her grief and doubts to rise to a new challenge. In the spring of 1885, she moved to her brother Natchez's ranch near Lovelock, Nevada. In that tiny community, Sarah began an unusual school to help her people.

At the time, the government ran "Indian schools" around the country. Their goal was to educate native

A Northern Paiute group harvests wild grass seeds in Lovelock, Nevada, in the 1890s.

boys and girls and teach them white men's ways. Sarah, though, had a different mission. She wanted her people to learn English, but she also wanted them to keep their own identity. As she explained in a letter to the Paiutes in California, her education plan would "fit your little ones for the battle of life, so that they can attend to their own affairs instead of having to call in a white man [for help]."

Sarah was a gifted teacher. Her young students enjoyed learning so much that they playfully scribbled English words on fences all around the town. Official visitors to her school observed that many of the students had learned more than white children their own age. Elizabeth Peabody, with her strong interest in education, was happy to send Sarah money to support the school. Yet the school's success was not enough to keep it going.

Government schools such as the Carlisle Industrial School for Indians in Pennsylvania had strict rules. Students were not allowed to wear native clothing, practice their traditions, or even speak their own languages. Often, children were given new English names. Punishment was swift and severe if a student disobeyed. Government officials thought they were helping students. Native people disagreed. Officials did not believe that native parents and children had the right or ability to decide what was best for themselves. Even though many Indian schools were far from their homes, some unhappy students ran away. Frequently, students who remained became seriously ill with diseases such as measles. Some died.

Lewis Hopkins died in October 1887 and is buried in Lovelock. He was 38.

Reservation officials pressured Paiute parents to send their children to government schools instead of Sarah's school. Sometimes, officials took the children away by force. Money was also a problem. Elizabeth Peabody was not wealthy. Other supporters of the school had doubts about how Sarah was using the funds they sent. They knew that her husband had gambled away donations before, and now he had re-entered her life.

However, Lewis was ill with tuberculosis, and he needed her help. She paid for his medical care and also gave him her emotional support. When Lewis died in 1887, Sarah mourned him as though they had never been apart. Following a custom of the time, she ordered memorial cards with a poem to express her feelings. Perhaps choosing to remember only the best about Lewis, Sarah chose this poem: "Tis hard to break the tender cord, When love has bound the heart."

Sarah herself had health problems. Now in her

40s, she suffered with rheumatism and from what was probably malaria. She experienced another heartbreak when, in 1889, lack of money and pupils forced her to close the school. Parents of her remaining students had begun to remove their children. They believed in the growing Ghost Dance movement, which promised a future where native people would not need to know English. Later that year, Sarah moved to Henry's Lake, Montana, now Idaho, to live with her sister Elma. In that isolated but beautiful countryside just west of what is now Yellowstone National Park, Sarah spent the few remaining years of her life.

Sarah's sister, Elma Smith, in 1919, the year before she died

Sarah Winnemucca is now honored for her achievements and courageous spirit. In 2005, the state of Nevada added a bronze statue of Sarah to Statuary Hall in the U.S. Capitol in Washington, D.C. A duplicate stands in the state Capitol in Carson City. Sarah's book inspired young Native American sculptor Benjamin Victor. He showed Sarah holding a book to represent her own writing and belief in education. She holds a shell flower to represent her pride in being Paiute. The way Sarah stands firmly as wind seems to sweep against her represents her strength.

Sarah lived long enough to read and hear about the terrible massacre of Ghost Dance followers at Wounded Knee Creek, South Dakota, in 1890. Sarah urged the Paiutes who lived near her to remain calm. She prevented their strong reactions from turning into further bloodshed.

On October 16, 1891, the 47-year-old "Paiute Princess" died. Sarah had suffered for years with different ailments, but the cause of her unexpected death remains a mystery. Her exact grave site is unknown. Her loyal brother Natchez risked the dangers of mountain travel in autumn to see her buried. Yet he arrived too late to see Sarah laid to rest.

Though some of her efforts failed, Sarah Winnemucca was a complicated person who achieved much. Some native people still have mixed feelings about her, but many respect her as well. Today, Sarah's reputation has grown. In 1993, the Nevada Writers Hall of Fame included her among its members. In 1994, citizens of Washoe

A bronze statue of Sarah Winnemucca stands in the Capitol in Carson City, Nevada. It is a duplicate of a statue in the U.S. Capitol.

County, Nevada, named a Reno elementary school in her honor. In 2005, a statue of Sarah Winnemucca was unveiled at the U.S. Capitol in Washington, D.C. It joined statues of other important people in Statuary Hall—a fitting tribute to a remarkable woman. ❧

Life and Times

WINNEMUCCA'S LIFE

1857

Lives with Major Ormsby's family in Genoa, Utah Territory, now Nevada, for a year

1844

Sarah Winnemucca is born in what is now western Nevada

1851

Travels to California with her grandfather, her mother, sisters, and brothers

1860

Pyramid Lake War takes place; Captain Truckee dies; Sarah attends convent school in California

1845

1855

1848

The Communist Manifesto by German writer Karl Marx is widely distributed

1846

German astronomer Johann Gottfried Galle discovers Neptune

1859

A Tale Of Two Cities by Charles Dickens is published

WORLD EVENTS

1864

Makes first stage
appearances in
Virginia City, Nevada,
and San Francisco,
California; reservations
at Pyramid Lake
and Walker River
become official

1865-66

Lives at Pyramid Lake
Reservation with
brother Natchez

1865

1863

Thomas Nast draws
the modern Santa
Claus for *Harper's
Weekly*, although Santa
existed previously

1865

The first fax is sent
from Lyon to Paris

WINNEMUCCA'S LIFE

1868-1871

Lives and works at Camp McDermit as an interpreter, scout, and hospital matron

1870

Writes letter on behalf of the Paiutes that is printed in newspapers and later published in Helen Hunt Jackson's book

1872

Marries Edward C. Bartlett

1870

1869

The periodic table of elements is invented by Dimitri Mendeleyev

1873

Typewriters get the QWERTY keyboard

WORLD EVENTS

1878

Works for the Army during the Bannock War and moves to the Yakima Reservation in Washington

1879

Lectures in San Francisco to publicize her people's plight

1876

Works as an interpreter at Malheur Reservation; marries Joseph Satwaller and leaves reservation

1875

1876

Alexander Graham Bell uses the first telephone to speak to his assistant, Thomas Watson

1877

German inventor Nikolaus A. Otto works on what will become the internal combustion engine for automobiles

1879

Electric lights are invented

WINNEMUCCA'S LIFE

1883
Begins tour of East Coast and gives more than 300 lectures; her book *Life Among the Piutes: Their Wrongs and Claims* is published

1881
Marries Lewis H. Hopkins

1880
Travels to Washington, D.C., with her father and brother to ask for her people's release from the reservation

1880

1881
The first Japanese political parties are formed

1884
The first practical fountain pen is invented by Lewis Edson Waterman, a 45-year-old American insurance broker

WORLD EVENTS

1885

Starts an Indian
school in Lovelock,
Nevada

1887

Witnesses her work
on the Dawes General
Allotment Act turn
into law by the U.S.
Congress; Lewis H.
Hopkins dies

1891

Dies at sister's home
in Henry's Lake,
Montana, now Idaho

1885

1890

1886

Grover Cleveland
dedicates the Statue
of Liberty in New
York, a gift from the
people of France

1893

Women gain voting
privileges in New
Zealand, the first
country to take
such a step

DATE OF BIRTH: About 1844

NATIVE NAME: Thocmetony (Shell Flower)

BIRTHPLACE: Near what is now Humboldt Lake, in western Nevada

FATHER: Winnemucca (1791?–1882)

MOTHER: Tuboitonie (?–1865)

EDUCATION: In household of Major Ormsby in Genoa, Utah Territory; briefly in convent school in San Jose, California; otherwise self-taught

SPOUSES: May have married a Paiute or white man in 1861 or 1862; married Edward Bartlett in 1872; married Joseph Satwaller in 1876; married Lewis Hopkins in 1881

DATE OF DEATH: October 16, 1891

PLACE OF BURIAL: Near Henry's Lake, Idaho

In the Library

Calabro, Marie. *The Perilous Journey of the Donner Party.* New York: Clarion, 1999.

Cooper, Michael L. *Indian School: Teaching the White Man's Way.* New York: Clarion, 1999.

Danneberg, Julie. *Amidst the Gold Dust: Women Who Forged the West.* Golden, Colo.: Fulcrum Resources, 2001.

Dolan, Edward F. *The American Indian Wars.* Brookfield, Conn.: The Millbrook Press, 2003.

Morrison, Dorothy Nafus. *Chief Sarah: Sarah Winnemucca's Fight for Indian Rights.* New York: Atheneum, 1980.

Scordato, Ellen, and W. David Baird. *Sarah Winnemucca: Northern Paiute Writer and Diplomat.* New York: Chelsea House, 1992.

Look for more Signature Lives books about this era:

James Beckwourth: *Mountaineer, Scout, and Pioneer*

Crazy Horse: *Sioux Warrior*

Geronimo: *Apache Warrior*

Sam Houston: *Texas Hero*

Bridget "Biddy" Mason: *From Slave to Businesswoman*

Zebulon Pike: *Explorer and Soldier*

On the Web

For more information on *Sarah Winnemucca*, use FactHound to track down Web sites related to this book.

1. Go to *www.facthound.com*
2. Type in a search word related to this book or this book ID: 0756510031
3. Click on the *Fetch It* button.

FactHound will find the best Web sites for you.

Historic Sites

Nevada State Museum
600 N. Carson St.
Carson City, NV 89701
775/687-4810
To visit the museum's Under One Sky exhibit about Nevada's Native American heritage and other exhibits

The Way It Was Museum
113 N. C St.
Virginia City, NV 89440
775/847-0766
To view a collection of Comstock Lode mining artifacts plus rare photographs and maps

aggressive
eager to fight or argue

allotment
a specific amount of something given to a person
or group

degrading
feeling useless, worthless, or bad

dismounted
removed oneself from a horse or piece of
equipment

eloquence
ability to speak easily with appropriate and
interesting words

epaulets
decorations on the shoulders of a soldier's coat

hypocrite
a person who does the opposite of what he or
she says

locks
an old-fashioned word for a person's hair

lode
an underground, large amount of a metal or mineral

massacre
the needless killing of a group of helpless people

ordeal
a painful or terrible experience

sarcasm
humor that points out someone's mistakes or
weaknesses

Source Notes

Chapter 1

Page 10, line 9: Gae Whitney Canfield. *Sarah Winnemucca of the Northern Paiutes.* Norman: University of Oklahoma Press, 1983, pp. 163-164.

Page 11, line 4: Ibid., pp. 163-164.

Page 13, line 5: Ibid., p. 167.

Chapter 2

Page 16, line 14: Sarah Winnemucca. *Life Among the Piutes: Their Wrongs and Claims.* Reno: University of Nevada Press, 1994 (first published 1883 by G.P. Putnam's Sons), p. 5.

Page 16, line 27: Time-Life Editors. *Indians of the Western Range.* Alexandria, Va.: Time- Life Books, 1995, p. 133.

Page 18, line 9: *Life Among the Piutes: Their Wrongs and Claims,* pp. 27-28.

Page 18, line 14: Ibid., p. 25.

Page 21, line 4: Ibid., p. 7.

Chapter 3

Page 23, line 7: Ibid., p. 25.

Page 24, line 6: Ibid., p.32.

Page 24, line 25: Ibid., p.29.

Page 26, line 17: Ibid., p. 42.

Page 28, line 25: Ibid., p. 63.

Chapter 4

Page 33, line 1: Sally Zanjani. *Sarah Winnemucca.* Lincoln: University of Nebraska Press, 2001, pp. 58-59.

Page 34, line 12: *Life Among the Piutes: Their Wrongs and Claims,* pp. 71-72.

Page 34, line 23: *Sarah Winnemucca,* p. 61.

Page 37, line 21: *Life Among the Piutes: Their Wrongs and Claims,* p. 47.

Chapter 5

Page 45, line 3: *Sarah Winnemucca of the Northern Paiutes,* p. 42.

Page 45, line 21: *Sarah Winnemucca,* pp. 76-77.

Page 47, line 3: *Life Among the Piutes: Their Wrongs and Claims,* p.78.

Page 47, line 19: Ibid., p. 78.

Chapter 6

Page 50, line 10: Ibid., pp. 86-87.

Page 51, line 5: Ibid., p. 82.

Page 52, line 21: Ibid., p. 82.

Page 54, line 3: Ibid., p. 85.

Page 56, line 4: *Sarah Winnemucca of the Northern Paiutes*, pp. 60-61.

Page 57, line 17: Ibid., p. 61.

Page 58, line 4: Ibid., p. 62.

Page 59, line 5: Ibid., p. 65.

Chapter 7

Page 64, line 3: *Sarah Winnemucca*, p. 111.

Page 64, line 6: Ibid., p. 111.

Page 66, line 2: *Life Among the Piutes: Their Wrongs and Claims*, p. 117.

Page 66, line 17: Ibid., p. 128.

Page 67, line 9: *Sarah Winnemucca*, p. 142.

Chapter 8

Page 71, line 6: *Life Among the Piutes: Their Wrongs and Claims*, p.164.

Page 73, line 3: Ibid., p. 164.

Page 73, line 9: Ibid., p. 193.

Page 75, line 4: Ibid., p. 205.

Page 75, line 8: Ibid., p. 205.

Page 77, line 4: Ibid., p. 239.

Chapter 9

Page 80, line 5: Ibid., p.222.

Page 81, line 19: Ibid., p. 236.

Page 87, line 10: Ibid., p. 207.

Chapter 10

Page 90, line 2: *Sarah Winnemucca*, p. 259.

Page 90, line 6: *Life Among the Piutes: Their Wrongs and Claims*, p. 12.

Page 91, line 9: *Sarah Winnemucca*, p. 267.

Page 92, line 25: *Sarah Winnemucca of the Northern Paiutes*, p. 253.

"American Experience: The Donner Party." Transcript of the PBS documentary retrieved online on September 24, 2004, from http://www.pbs.org/wgbh/amex/donner/filmmore/pt.html.

"Artist Sought for Nevada Statue of Sarah Winnemucca." *Reno Gazette-Journal.* July 25, 2003. Retrieved online on August 28, 2004.

Ashby, Ruth, and Deborah Gore Ohrn. *Herstory: Women Who Changed the World.* New York: Viking, 1995.

Bush, John. "The History of the Virginia and Truckee Railroad." Retrieved October 1, 2004, from http://www.vcnevada.com/history/Vnthist.htm.

Canfield, Gae Whitney. *Sarah Winnemucca of the Northern Paiutes.* Norman: University of Oklahoma Press, 1983.

Egan, Ferol. *Sand in a Whirlwind: The Paiute Indian War of 1860.* Garden City, N.Y.: Doubleday, 1972.

Gardner, Sheila. "'Pink Tea' Aims to Get Sarah Winnemucca in the U.S. Capitol." *Reno Gazette-Journal.* April 21, 2003. Retrieved online on August 28, 2004.

Kilcup, Karen L., ed. *Native American Women's Writing, 1800-1924: An Anthology.* Malden, Mass.: Blackwell, 2000.

Ritchie, Joy S., and Kate Ronald, eds. *Available Means: An Anthology of Women's Rhetoric(s).* Pittsburgh: University of Pittsburgh Press, 2001.

Rose, Mary. "Sarah Winnemucca: A Voice of Reason and Compassion in Difficult Times." *The Columbian.* January 31, 1999. Retrieved August 28, 2004, from http://www.columbian.com.

Ruoff, A. LaVonne Brown. "Early Native American Women Authors: Jane Johnston Schoolcraft, Sarah Winnemucca, S. Alice Callahan, E. Pauline Johnson, and Zitkala-Sa." In *Nineteenth-Century American Women Writers: A Critical Reader,* edited by Karen L. Kilcup. Malden, Mass.: Blackwell Publishers, 1998.

"Sarah Winnemucca." University of Nevada Web site. Retrieved August 20, 2004, from http://www.unr.edu/wrc/nwhp/biograph/winnemucca.htm.

Senier, Siobhan. *Voices of American Indian Assimilation and Resistance: Helen Hunt Jackson, Sarah Winnemucca, and Victoria Howard.* Norman: University of Oklahoma Press, 2001.

Time-Life Editors. *Chroniclers of Indian Life.* Alexandria, Va.: Time-Life Books, 1996.

Time-Life Editors. *Indians of the Western Range.* Alexandria, Va.: Time-Life Books, 1995.

Walker, Cheryl. *Indian Nation: Native American Literature and Nineteenth Century Nationalisms.* Durham, N.C.: Duke University Press, 1997.

Winnemucca, Sarah. *Life Among the Piutes: Their Wrongs and Claims.* Reno: University of Nevada Press, 1994. First published 1883 by G.P. Putnam's Sons.

Zanjani, Sally. *Sarah Winnemucca.* Lincoln: University of Nebraska Press, 2001.

Natalie M. Rosinsky is the award-winning author of more than 90 publications, including 10 books about Native American tribes. She writes about science, history, economics, social studies, and popular culture. One of her two cats usually sits near her computer as she works in Mankato, Minnesota. Natalie earned graduate degrees from the University of Wisconsin and has been a high school teacher and college professor as well as a corporate trainer.

Image Credits